All Marketing Is Local

The Social Selling Edition

Written by John Meyer

Cover Illustration by Justin Meyer

All Marketing is Local - A common sense approach to marketing your business.

Tip O'Neil was Speaker of the House during the presidencies of Gerald Ford, Jimmy Carter and Ronald Reagan. He said "All politics is local." "We can start solving national problems by making connections at our own grassroots level". "Because," he said, "all politics is local."

The key word is "connections". National advertising and marketing can be great, but if it isn't connecting with your local customer it is not working.

I always come back to a vision from the 1950's of two neighbor women talking over the waist high fence. They're talking about everything from what's new with the family to their favorite store, car and dish soap. That is true word of mouth marketing and truly reinforces that all marketing is local.

This edition of All Marketing Is Local has been updated with aspects of Social Media, and how leveraging the power of social selling can help get to word of mouth much quicker.

Table of Contents

Introduction:

Thank you to my wife Meg and my son Justin. I could not have done this without your encouragement and support.

This will be somewhat of an interactive book. As you are reading the book you will be getting ideas on how you might be able to apply some of the things in the book with your own marketing and business development efforts.

From time to time I will ask you a question.

First question. Please think of your favorite restaurant. Now write it down here or on a notepad that you can come back to later.

____

As you read this book I have my own goal. You should be able to write down at least 5 ideas that you will apply to your marketing and business development efforts.

The idea that all marketing is local is pretty common sense. It goes back to neighbors talking over the fence. Word of mouth is the best form of marketing. What a great (and free) way to get people talking about your products and company. Now that fence that people talked over has also become email marketing and social media with Twitter, Facebook, LinkedIn, YouTube, and Instagram to name a few.

We will look at all aspects of marketing; all traditional means of marketing as well as digital, online, and social ways to market your business, products and services.

This book will look at those aspects through a dartboard type of target. The bullseye represents what we strive for: Free word of Mouth. I hope to give you some ideas on how to leverage your word of mouth with traditional and digital marketing. Going outward from that bull's-eye are the other aspects of marketing and their costs, as well as effectiveness. The great thing about online marketing is you can really track ROI (Return on Investment) much easier than with traditional media like TV, Radio, Print ads, and Direct mail.

All components can have a valuable addition to your marketing and business development plan. But how do you know which ones to use?

You need to think about your customers. Who are they, where do they go to get information? Twitter, Instagram and Pinterest may be very popular overall in social marketing, but it doesn't necessarily mean that is the place you should be for marketing. Or maybe it is. You need to really think about what I call the "sphere of influence". Where people go to learn, interact and gather information. That will help you decide where your marketing dollars, and time, will be best spent.

Good luck.
John Meyer

Chapter One – Getting Through the Clutter

Marketing Overload: Getting your brand through the clutter.

Here is a question for you. How many commercial messages does an average consumer receive each day?

If we look at our marketing target, how do we use the various marketing techniques to get your message through the marketing clutter that exists today? What do I mean by "marketing clutter"? Here is another little homework/worksheet/thought process. Think about your day, from the time you wake up to the time you go to bed, how many product brands do you see? How many brand messages do you hear about?

Maybe you wake up to a clock radio that has a logo on it, the radio station you listen to promotes its call-in number, and you hear a few commercials before the next song. You get up and brush your teeth. The toothpaste has a brand, your soap and shampoo have a brand, your clothes have a brand. You check your Facebook, Twitter, Instagram and LinkedIn feeds. You drive your kids to school and see branded cars, perhaps a billboard or two. Off to work you see other billboards, hear a few more ads. You stop at Starbucks and get a brand of coffee. ☺ Read through the paper, online or print, and see multiple ads. You check your social media feeds again! Go to lunch and see more ads, your menu has the restaurant name. And as you drive you are listening to the radio and hear more commercials.

On your way home you stop at the grocery store; brands upon brands upon brands on the store shelves. Just think about what you see at a large department store.

You come home after work and watch some TV, commercials, unless you TIVO (that's another part of this book☺). Then you do some work on your computer, check your LinkedIn, Twitter, and Facebook accounts again, ads, ads, ads.

You get the idea.

The answer to the question: In 2017 Forbes reported somewhere between 4000 and 10,000 is the number that represents just how many commercial messages an average consumer receives each day.

How do you get your message through the clutter? It can be a challenge but the first thing you should do is set some goals. What are your business goals? How can marketing help you reach and exceed your goals? When you are doing your marketing, you need to be able to track your results as best you can and learn from your efforts.

Another thing that may help you: Do you have a marketing mentor? Someone in your life that you have been impressed with their business? Feel free to ask her if she would be a mentor and if you can ask her questions from time to time.

You can also get ideas or mentors from organizations. Join a local chapter of the Business Marketing Association or American Marketing Association. If you are on LinkedIn you can join groups that are marketing related and get ideas there as well and ask questions. Follow some of your favorite writers Twitter handles.

You should have your business marketing goals in mind. When you are writing down your goals make sure they are SMART! I learned about SMART goals years ago while managing a software sales team.   The first known uses of the term occur in the November 1981 issue of *Management Review* by George T. Doran

"My marketing plan will make me successful" … is not a good goal. Here is why:

S = Specific

M = Measurable - "What will success look like?"

A = Achievable – Goals should be challenging but not unrealistic.

R = Results Oriented - Measure results, not merely the steps you take.

T = Time Specific – Goals are often long term, but set milestones and check points.

What are your marketing and business goals? Are they SMART? Here are a few examples:

- 100 new clients by the end of the month, quarter, year.
- Open 10 new locations by the end of the year.

- Reduce Marketing Expenses by 10%, Improve ROI by 15% by the end of the fiscal year.

- Keep track of how new clients hear about my business.

- Start an email newsletter by the end of the month. Send a newsletter each month. Have specific goals for the newsletter.

- Update website within two months. What are my goals of the website?

- Start a Facebook page within a month and update it daily.

- Start a "refer a friend" or "customer loyalty" program by the end of the 1st quarter of the New Year.

- Target a local magazine that my customers/potential customers read and determine how I can leverage it; print ads? Ask to write a column and become a SME (subject matter expert), become involved with local events hosted by the magazine. Pitch a story to a writer.

- Track my marketing results monthly, quarterly, yearly.

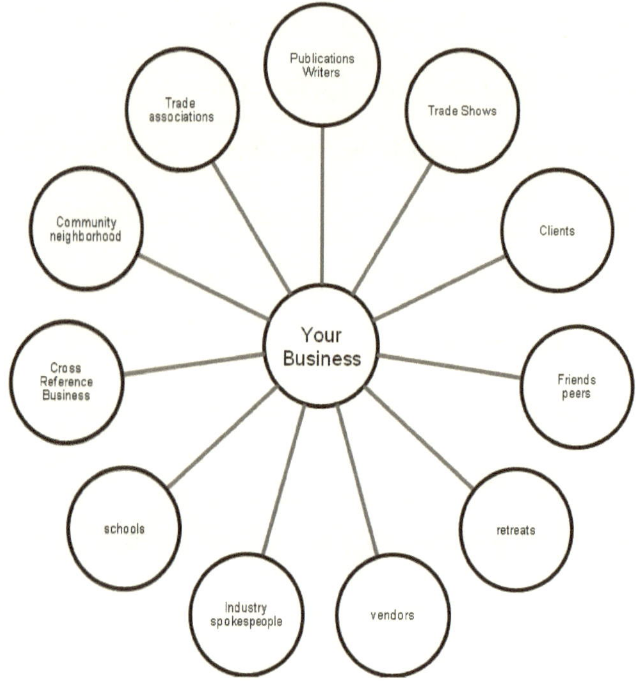

Your Company's Sphere of Influence

When determining what type of marketing channels you want to use you should first put together a "sphere of influence". A sphere of influence is the different places and organizations that your clients and potential clients go to where they could potentially hear about you and learn more about you. Both in person and online/social media.

Take a moment to write down some of your own ideas. You may have fewer numbers of influence points or more. Find some quiet time where you can think about where you can meet new customers. Where will you find your "target market"?

Cross Reference Business – these are companies that are in your neighborhood, or sphere of influence that you could do some co marketing activities with. It could be as simple as each business having some flyers or brochures available when your customers walk through the door.

Trade Shows – these can be local or national trade shows that your target customer would attend. More about trade shows in Chapter five.

You get the idea. Putting this sphere of influence together will help you when you are determining where you will spend your time and money.

Cost of Influence:

You have put your thoughts down and may have drawn your own diagram on your sphere of influence.

Now I will talk a little more about the "bullseye" I mentioned earlier.

Here is another diagram I call the "Cost of Influence"

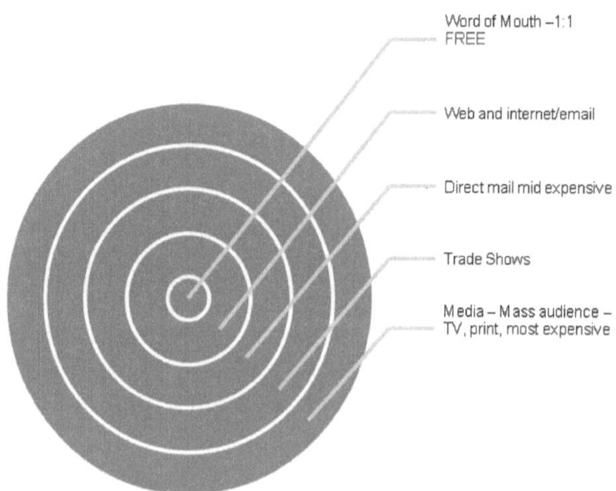

Cost of Influence

This diagram visually shows you the "dart board" with the bullseye in the center. Word of mouth is the best form of marketing you can ever receive. One of your happy customers is referring you to another person. You have a new client based on the opinion of your customer telling their friend that if they are in the market for your type of product or service they should choose you. It doesn't get any better than that!

I know some businesses where that is their only form of marketing; Referrals from existing clients. You can't always rely on that happening. You may have to create an incentive program for your clients to talk about you.

One of the things I want this book to point out is that in every aspect of marketing there can be a "local angle"; TV, print, email, etc. Whether it is leveraging a local TV station's "Best of Town", a local magazine or newspapers "best of town", leveraging your own expertise in a local magazine article, or leveraging other marketing tools to give you a leg up. This book is designed for you to make SMART marketing decisions that help you gain new clients and keep them happy and referring you to their friends. This could be as simple as liking your Facebook page.

Let's review…

Chapter Two - Mass Media

How do you get your message through the clutter? As I said before, knowing who your audience is can help quite a bit. If you have a product that can be used by most people, or you want it to be, you may think of getting it "out to the masses" through television and radio. Your budget may not allow TV. Let's look at one example.

Television:

One ad I have always found intriguing is the 1984 "Apple Macintosh" super bowl ad that was shown at halftime during the super bowl game. Go to Bing or Google and search "Apple 1984 ad". It was shown on broadcast TV only one time.

The commercial depicts in gray colors an Orwellian community with a large audience watching a giant screen with a video of an old man telling them what to do. In runs a young woman in colorful shorts and tank top swinging a small sledge hammer. She runs to the stage and throws the hammer into the screen. It shatters and Apple announces a new way to compute and why "1984 won't be like 1984". Apple Macintosh.

It was a very creative television commercial, and cost a small fortune since it ran at halftime in 1984. Just think what a super bowl ad would cost today? The ad won awards. But did it sell more Macintosh? Today Macintosh is about 9-10% market share of the personal computer industry. Not bad when you look at their stock price and the other products they have. That ad didn't make them the #1 personal computer manufacturer, but did it lead the way for Apple the company to be known for creating "totally cool" products? Think iPod, iPhone, iTunes, and iPad. The ad was but one thing in Apples repertoire of marketing tools. And very expensive. The PR that happened around the ad was probably more beneficial than the ad itself.

The cool thing with today's internet technology is maybe you don't need TV. That ad is still on YouTube and can be seen every day by people who are most interested. How could you leverage YouTube and have a video of your company and service and get people to watch it? Amplify the video through social media? We'll discuss internet tools in a later chapter.

Let's talk a little more about TV. Earlier when I reviewed some of the ads you might see during a day I talked about watching Television in the evening after work. Many people now use TIVO or DVRs (Digital Video Recorders). Record your favorite show and watch it at your leisure and skip the commercials! Ouch say the ad agencies who work tirelessly trying to create the newest, coolest "Apple ad". Ouch say the marketing departments of companies spending millions upon millions of dollars on TV ads.

MediaPost reports an estimated 92% of TV ads are being skipped over." Who is your audience? Do they have a DVR? Do you care? Can you afford TV commercials? And if so can you still grab people's attention as they fast forward through the ads?

What are the alternative ways you can look to leverage TV in a creative way? Does it make sense for you to advertise in a local market on the local news casts, on the local PBS stations? Local cable channels? Or are there ways to have the local news do a story about you and your business?

You can get detailed information about TV viewers at arbitron.com. Go to the "Free Studios and Reports" section for a lot of terrific information you can use to review what may work for you in TV.

Better yet think of ways you can get on TV for free. Get someone to interview you about your product or service. A little free publicity can go a long way. Do any of the local TV stations or radio stations have a contest for the "best of" that your company could participate in? If not, can you create one? Best Health Club, Best Restaurant, Best Florist, etc. Local magazines and newsletters often do these stories as well. Then when it happens you can utilize another great marketing tool to get your customers to vote for you. Send then email newsletters saying you are in the running and to please vote and to please forward the newsletter to a friend so they can vote for you too. Talk about it on your social media pages like Facebook. You may even pick up more clients just from that. I get ahead of myself as I devote whole chapters to leveraging email marketing as well as social media.

Estimates are that people who use a DVR skip 50-70% of the ads. I know in our family if we have a "TIVO'd" show we skip 100% of the ads.

Many people now watch some of their favorite shows on YouTube or hulu. YouTube is also a great place to start your own Channel that can be linked to your homepage on your website. You can then post different video links on your social media channels.

Radio

What about local radio? That's another very interesting marketing tool. Radio was supposed to die after TV came out in the 1940s and 1950s. Radio was supposed to die after the growth of the internet and web sites. Wait a minute, it is still a very strong medium.

Whether you are listening to your favorite talk radio while driving to work or lunch, listening to relaxing music on your favorite FM station while at work, or listening to satellite radio, there are several aspects that you may be able to take advantage of.

It's pretty easy to check out what your local AM and FM stations carry. And how does that tie in with your business? Country stations may have a good tie in with companies that participate with local stock shows or rodeos. A local FM station may have a tie in with your company.

Similar to TV stations the radio stations in your area may have a "Best of" contest where listeners are asked to call in or go to the radio website to vote for their favorite restaurant, day spa, shipping store, health club, etc.

Go to arbitron.com and you can get a plethora of information about radio. They even have statistics broken down by demographics; Hispanic radio, black radio, public radio.

News/talk/information is rated the #1 format according to Arbitran's Radio Today (you can download this free report at Arbitron.com). Country is rated #2 overall and #1 for music choice.

Do you own a sporting goods store? Maybe there is a way to get a promotion going with an all sports talk show. Cosponsor an event the station covers/sponsors.

At a local level the advertising costs may not be too expensive for the market and time you are advertising. You can check out what types of promotions you might get involved with at a much lower cost. Or be so bold as to talk with the radio station to host a segment, be a guest speaker, and be an authority that the radio station goes to when they want to get expert advice and opinions on the air. You can also leverage the radio station's Twitter handle and other social media to help promote.

Chapter Three - Print Advertising

In this day and age of digital marketing, should print advertising be a part of your marketing mix? Maybe. Overall, I think advertising is good if you have the budget, and it fits in with your goals, as it can build your brand. But don't expect immediate results as it takes time for ads to "work".

"You have to run an ad twenty seven times against one individual before it has its desired impact. Why? Because only one out of nine ads is seen, and you've got to see it at least three times before it sinks in."
-Jay Levinson, Marketing Guru

Magazines:

Next time you are in a Barnes & Noble or your local grocery store check out the magazine section.

That is just the tip of the iceberg for the number of magazines there are in the United States alone. That does not include the thousands of local and regional magazines designed for local community news. There are thousands of magazine titles out there. Some of the news magazines may be declining, but some niche magazines are growing. Ask yourself where your customer is? Bridal magazines are huge and growing, with over 100 different titles.

Cat Fancy, Guitars, Personal Computers, Gaming, Brides, Railroad Magazines, Teen magazines, Travel Magazines, Political, Arts and Crafts, are just a sampling of some of the magazines that are out there.

The question should not be, should print be a part of your advertising? The question should be, what magazines does your target audience read? Again, all marketing is local. Maybe your customers are people within your community. Perhaps the local community newspaper or regional magazine is a good fit. Maybe you have a higher end clientele and the luxury city magazine is appropriate. Do you have a business that has customers nationally and there could be a national magazine that would work for you? Maybe there are national "niche" magazines that would be a better fit for you. Many times, these are trade magazines related to the business you are in. They also all leverage social media.

Whenever I look at magazines for possible advertising, I see what other things they offer. Do they have a web site that you can also get an ad on as part of your marketing mix? Maybe the magazine has an event they do that you can also get involved in. If they have an active web site do they also have an email newsletter you can leverage? Do they have a community page on their website where you can add your company website address and you then have a link to them on your site? We'll talk more about SEO and "free links" in Chapter eight.

If they are on Facebook or Twitter how can you leverage that? There will be more about that in the chapter about Social Media.

You may be able to negotiate a better price for your advertising by combining all the different aspects you may want to take advantage of. Be sure to ask about package deals.

I live in the Denver area and the high-end city magazine is 5280. Get it? Denver is a mile high. You can check it out at 5280.com to see what they have to offer. With 5280 there are other avenues of advertising along with print ads. They have various online ads, advertiser links (good for building your free listings in SEO), as well as a potential area for Market place listings. It is a luxury magazine so the rates reflect that. It may be good if you have a restaurant, wellness center, or other high-end company and clients that read the magazine. You should also research to see if these magazines have a "best of town" edition. Get your business listed and try to win top honors. You can also leverage their social media. As of September 2018, the 5280 magazine has 244,000 Twitter followers. What a great way to promote your message on Twitter and include their Twitter handle.

Many communities have regional magazines and newspapers. One near where I live is called Colorado Serenity. It offers articles about things going on in the area, and many local businesses advertise in it as it is indeed very targeted. The advertising rates are much less expensive as well, and it has a very niche social media following.

Print advertising can possibly be a part of your marketing mix, especially if you are leveraging every way possible for a "local" angle. One way would be to become a subject matter expert and write an ongoing column.

There are some out there that don't believe branding money towards print ads is very useful.

"Virtually all branding money is totally wasted."

-Seth Godin, Author of Permission Marketing

Seth Godin is one of my favorite authors around marketing. That quote is from his book "Permission Marketing, Turning Strangers Into Friends, And Friends Into Customers". I'll talk more about some of his ideas when we discuss email marketing.

Here are statistics Seth put together about why he feels this way:

- Typical National Advertising Magazine (Time, Newsweek or People) – cost of a full-page color ad $50,000 for a circulation of 3,000,000

- Number of minutes spent per issue: 22

- Number of Ads per issue: 80

- Even with no articles that is 16 seconds per ad. We know that most people do read articles and don't read ads.

- Percentage of people who remember your ad? Maybe 8%. It's a Seth guess.

- Percentage who read the ad and can recall: 30%

- Number impacted: 72,000. Cost of impacting each person is 80 cents.

It doesn't sound too rosy does it? Not if you don't have much of a budget, and you really need to run ads for a year or two to get the branding done. But of course, these statistics are for a national ad campaign. Your best bet may be to leverage local, or niche, magazines' marketing and advertising (and their social media followers) to help build your brand.

All aspects of marketing are pieces of your marketing mix. Maybe it doesn't make sense to have any print ads. It all depends on what works and what doesn't work.

If you decide to incorporate print ads in your campaign I would recommend three things:

1. Don't advertise solely to "build brand". Have you ever seen ads that try to build brand with no call to action and

no web site to gather more information? In all of your advertising try to incorporate a call to action (CTA) asking people to go to your web site. It may be for a free trial of your product, to sign up for a contest, to watch a demonstration of what your services can offer, or download a free white paper or eBook. It may sound silly but include your website URL address. Some people actually forget this. You can also ask people to follow you on your social media channels.

2. Try to always incorporate a testimonial from one of your happy clients. It adds some clarity if you have a nice testimonial along with the person and company who gave you the quote. If you are a B2B marketer include the person's name and the company name. It means more to see the person's name and the company name, as well as city and state versus Joe B from Illinois.

3. If you do decide to run some print ads, spend the extra money it costs to hire an ad agency or brand manager who will do a very appealing job of representing your company's brand, your image. Do it yourself ads don't quite cut it when you are trying to build your professional image.

When and if you decide to do print advertising in magazines look through the magazines you think about. See what the ads look like that are in there. Is there a section in the back of the magazine for smaller ads? And is it a magazine that you may want to call directly and pitch an idea for an article you would like to write. Again, the more local the magazine the better your chances are of this. It's a matter of leveraging a marketing outlet without having to spend the marketing dollars for an ad. Become a local subject matter expert and start an ongoing column.

Newspapers

Wow, what can I say about newspapers? I try to write about what I know and to be honest this is the one area that I have done little. We gave up our subscription to our daily paper a few years ago. I get so much information from the newspaper website and other news sources, I am one of the millions that are giving up on a printed version of a newspaper. Advertisers are too. That is why you see several newspapers across the country going out of business.

Newspaper print advertising has been hit the hardest with the new digital age. The difference I see with Magazines and Newspapers is that magazines can be so niche related that people still like getting them, holding them and reading in their house, at the hair salon, etc. With newspapers more and more people are getting their news from websites and may not even go to the newspaper web sites.

Some companies still spend a small fortune advertising in newspapers. If it works, great. You will still see the car ads, the furniture and mattress ads, and of course the Sunday coupons.

Chapter Four – Direct Mail

Let's start with some statistics about direct mail.

The normal response rate is 1%. That is considered a "good" response rate for direct mail. Just think of all the post cards and letters you throw into the trash as you sort through your mail. Are your prospective customers doing the same thing?

The average direct mail piece costs between $2.00 and $3.00. That includes the design, production, postage. Say you have 500 people on your prospect list you are mailing to. That is $1000 to $1500 for maybe 5 people responding to the message. That may be a good ROI if what you are selling is really expensive.

Just like all marketing, direct mail may be a good component to your marketing mix. I still believe in some instances where direct mail is very appropriate. Maybe you want to send your clients a birthday card, an anniversary card, invitation to a special event, or special announcements.

In this day and age, it really is nice to get a personal birthday card via "snail mail" versus another email. A personally written message in a note card can go a long way.

I have a rule of thumb for direct mail. The colder the prospect, the easier it should be to see your message. Send a post card and not a letter with an envelope. The envelope will get thrown in the trash without even seeing your message inside. At least with a post card they will see your brand, your logo and hopefully a thoughtful quick message to get their attention, and a call to action to visit your web site!

Another rule of thumb is to clean your mailing list and test it. If you are planning to buy some lists from a broker, get references that they are reputable. Make sure the list is clean; includes zip codes, and full name instead of "Dear Occupant".

If you are planning a fancier mailing, I would strongly suggest sending a postcard first. The post card can get your message out as well, and in many instances it's better because again the recipient does not have to open an envelope. Send the postcard to the list and make sure your card has your return address on it.

Then when you get the undeliverable from the post office, you can go in and delete those addresses from your database, so you are sending the more expensive mailing to a clean list. If you have the resources you can also hire a 3rd party to clean the database for you, verify addresses and make sure that the people still work there.

Make sure you have a goal for your mailing. What is the call to action? Go to your website? Call a phone number? Both? It is always a good idea to have someone that hasn't been working on it proof read your message. Who, what, when, where, why, and how is always a good rule to follow. Who is your desired audience? What is the call to action? Where do they go to follow up with you? Why is it worth their while to do so (may be a limited time offer), and how do they take advantage of your offer.

What are the goals for the mailing? Ten new clients? One hundred products sold? Review each campaign to see what's working and what can be improved. Keep statistics when reviewing your goals of how many new clients came to you from:

email, direct mail, word of mouth, website, etc. You can ask your new clients this in person or online if that is how they sign up.

Proof read it once more. I have learned from personal experience that if the website is spelled incorrectly or the phone number is off by a digit you've just flushed those marketing dollars down the toilet. Oops.

If you are on a limited budget for your post card mailing, there are a lot of pretty easy to use and inexpensive tools out there. One that comes to mind is vistaprint.com. They have many templates available. If it is something you want a little fancier or customized you can work with the same ad agency that helped you design your web site, or your print ads to have the same look to your post cards as your website. At a minimum keep your logo consistent.

To keep the local angle, include a testimonial and name of one of your clients. Be sure to ask them for permission to use their name.

Don't expect one direct mail piece and one mailing to do the trick. You may want to do a direct mail campaign once a month for several months to get your message out there. During the first and second month your postcard may go in the trash. But the third month the recipient may take another look and decide to respond to your call to action.

Some companies will also use post card mailings to alert their customers that they are starting an email newsletter and to please go to their website and sign up for it. Email marketing is a whole chapter in itself, but is considered direct mail.

Many companies mail long letters and catalogues. I still don't understand why they don't send something that is much shorter and to the point with call to action to the website. That can be a virtual catalogue, flyer, business proposition.

Some companies still want to send a printed newsletter. Why I ask? It is so expensive and wastes so much paper. I recommend doing a nice email newsletter whenever possible. To each his own. Some people do enjoy getting a hard copy newsletter. It would be a good idea to do a survey of your customers. Do they enjoy the paper version or would they prefer an email newsletter.

I am a member of a nonprofit organization and they send both. I am still trying to talk them into doing just the email version. Of course, their point is that their audience does not all use email. So that is a good point. You don't want to ignore the small percentage of your audience (and getting smaller) that may not use email.

One more thing about direct mail. Make sure you have a follow-up plan in place. I recently did a high end B2B direct mail campaign where the sales team was targeting 100 specific people in companies they are trying to get into. We did a lot of prep beforehand with the inside sales team and sale executives. We made sure we had the right contact information. We knew exactly when the pieces were delivered so the inside sales team knew when to do the follow-up for the goal of setting up a meeting. It was a very successful campaign with high ROI due to the pre and post planning and setting goals.

Chapter Five – Trade Shows

I Love Trade Shows! I Hate Trade Shows!

Which category do you fall in?

Trade shows come in all shapes and sizes and target audiences. Everything from your local (there's that local word again) chamber of commerce or community event with a dozen or so booths and a couple hundred attendees to the largest of the large like the Consumer Electronics Show in Las Vegas. The January 2009 show I attended had over 2500 exhibitors with booth areas as large as a football field and 100,000 people attended the event. These are lower numbers from the year before due to a slow economy! According to the Las Vegas Sun CES covered 1.7 million square feet of exhibit space between the Las Vegas Convention Center, The Sands Expo and Convention Center, the Venetian and the Las Vegas Hilton.

I walked the floor of that show as an attendee about 6 years ago and was blown away by just how big it was. I prefer smaller niche-oriented shows.

Personally, I love trade shows. They can be a wonderful way to meet prospects and visit with existing clients to bring you new prospects/clients. Trade shows are great because it's a place where your prospective customers come to network and learn.

I have been at trade shows and have heard other vendors complain because "nobody is coming to my booth", "what a slow show", "my feet hurt". If your feet hurt take a walk around the trade show floor and introduce yourself to the other exhibitors. Maybe there is a partnership in the making out there somewhere where you can help each other's business. If the show seems slow, figure out how you could make it seem to go faster by doing other things around the show. If nobody is coming to your booth whose fault is that? Yours.

Here are some really great ways to leverage trade shows so that they are always productive. Don't get me wrong, some trade shows are better than others, and over time you will learn which ones are the best to participate in.

Before I sign up for a tradeshow, I review how I can market before the trade show, during the trade show, and after the tradeshow.

If you just buy a trade show spot and expect people to flock to your booth, by the end of the day or week (however long the show is) you will be complaining about your sore feet.

Before The Trade Show:

Research the trade shows that you are thinking of attending. What does the show offer around the event that you could participate in? Many trade shows are actually part of a larger convention where many speakers and seminars occur.

Find out how you go about becoming a speaker for the next show. If you are a Subject Matter Expert in your field let people know it. The presentation should not be a sales pitch for your company but a presentation around what you are an expert about (thought leadership). Obviously, it's a good way to meet people 1:1 and many will follow-up with you either after the seminar or come to your booth for more information.

What types of trade show packages do they offer? Advertising in show guides, sponsorships, social media activity plans, and attendee lists are things that I look for in order to make the entire event worthwhile. Do they offer links to your website on their website? As an exhibitor do you also have the opportunity to attend the seminar sessions? Do they host round tables where you can volunteer at running the discussion? What does the floor plan look like for the exhibitors? What flexibility do you have in having your booth where you want it? At some shows it is good to be up near the front. I have been to other shows where it doesn't matter.

What kinds of activities does the show put on to get attendees into the exhibit hall? Host breakfast and lunches? Cocktail hours? Games? Any opportunities where you can give a pitch in a sit-down venue?

Some events offer exhibitors a pre-conference RSVP list of people who have signed up for the event. Many have the street address as well as email. I would be extremely careful about sending an email to the attendees prior to the show… because every other exhibitor will be sending an email as well and most of those emails never get opened. You may not want to spend the money to send a direct mail piece to all attendees inviting them to your booth with an amazing offer.

When they offer this list, I look through it and see who is attending. Are some of the attendees people I'd like my company to meet with? Instead of sending something to everyone you can target those who you would really like to meet with and send them an introduction letter as well as follow-up with a personal phone call. This can be great to add to any ABM (Account Based Marketing) plans you have. Let them know you will be at the exhibit hall and to look for you.

You can send a postcard to the entire list about your company and a call to action to visit your booth. Promote a fun prize you will be giving away. Then send a personal letter to the folks you really want to talk to and follow that up with a phone call. You can also add all the names to your prospect database and start an ongoing campaign with them as well.

When reviewing the list see if it includes vendors as well as attendees. You don't want to send information to fellow exhibitors, especially if some of them are your competitors.

My two cents about this: Do NOT tell them to "come to booth #123". Booth numbers are for vendors to find their space and set up their trade show booth. Once it is set up the booth number is covered up. Most trade shows (another thing to research) will have maps of the trade show with your Company name listed. They may also have the numbers in a way you can be found. But don't depend on that.

You should send an email to your existing clients and let them know you will be at the trade show. Many of them may attend and it's always good to visit with your existing clients. Ask them to introduce them to others they meet there. Many companies have an "events" section on their website so people can see what trade shows they are attending.

If you are not detail oriented (a nice word for OCD, and I mean that in a positive way) hire someone to manage the logistics of the trade show process; filling out the paperwork, shipping the booth material, setting up your booth, getting literature and giveaways sent, managing leads, etc.

During The Trade Show

Have a booth that reflects your brand, it may look like your web site. Have an image and your message at head height so when people walk by they can glance at your booth and see what you offer. It is similar to an ad in a magazine. People flip the page in the magazine and the person walking by your booth has just passed the booth by you and is about to go to the booth on the other side of you. So, your booth should grab their attention and let them know what you do.

Have a table cloth that has your logo and brand message hanging over the table.

Make any handouts short and simple. Trade show cards are fine to have your message and website and phone number. Don't hand out a ton of literature to everyone. It will end up in the hotels trash can because people go through their trade show bags as they pack and most of the stuff they've collected goes in the trash.

Many people who attend shows have children and will sometimes collect things that they can give their kids when they get home. Have a simple but fun giveaway. It can be as simple as a fun pen with your message and website on it. There are many companies out there like pens.com that offer all kinds of "trash and trinkets" for fun giveaways and are fairly inexpensive. If you work with a consultant or agency they will have some ideas as well.

You may want to have some more expensive and nicer giveaways on hand for people who really seem interested and talk to you for a while. Also have some additional information for them if interested. In most cases get their business card and send them the information when you get back to your office. If you have sales teams to follow-up give them these leads first.

Don't tackle people that walk by your booth. I always laugh at trade shows when I see these people who stand in the aisle with their handout and "get in your space" and hand you a flyer and ask if you are interested in XYZ. Try to have activities INSIDE YOUR BOOTH that get people interested in talking to you. Have fun giveaways, have a very fun contest where people have to answer a question, fill out a form (or attach business card), and have people work your booth who are knowledgeable about your products and are very engaging.

Here is a fun contest idea: Get a martini glass. Fill it up with M&Ms (or your favorite candy) and have the contest be "How many M&Ms are in the Martini Glass" Guess the closest number and win a prize. Make sure there is a lid or saran wrap on the top so people don't eat a few while they are trying to figure it out.

Make sure the prize is fun. Everybody loves Apple products. They come in various price points. What I really like about them is when you order them you can have them engraved with your message and website address.

When you do have the opportunity to talk to someone give them your "elevator pitch" of what you do. A sentence or two of what your company offers. A lot of times people are just walking thru the expo hall seeing who's there on their way to their next seminar. That way you get your message out. If they need to go they at least have that message. If they have more time you can discuss your products and solutions in more detail. Be sure to get their business card and make note of their specific interest. This way you have good data to follow-up with once you or your sales team is back in the office.

Be careful of the people who will literally talk to you for an hour and turns out they are the decision maker's brother-in-law's cousin. Clarify who you are talking to upfront and make sure your time is spent wisely.

Try to plan some meetings while at the trade show with existing clients, either at your booth or offsite. Also, try to stay at the hotel that hosts the event. It's a great place for networking.

The busier the show is, the faster the time flies. Your feet will get tired one way or another. Wear comfortable shoes. Always have your booth staffed so that when things are a bit slow people can take break and walk around to get some exercise. I enjoy walking around the trade show floor to see who else is there and who has great trade show booths. There are some you know right away what they do and others that you have no clue what they do.

Business cards. Make sure your business card is a marketing tool as well. Is one side blank? Spend the few extra bucks and have your branding message on that side as well, or a customer testimonial.

Customer dinners. If you know some of your customers will be attending the event ask them if you can buy them dinner, breakfast, a cup of coffee. It's good for the ongoing service of your clients and they will be more inclined to introduce you to other people at the event that could become future clients.

My trade show pet peeve. Chairs in the Booth. Just say no. Your staff should be standing and ready to talk to people as they come to your booth. If people are sitting down that sends a message to people who walk by that "I am tired and I do not want to talk to you". Again, have breaks available so staff can go somewhere and sit down, have lunch, catch up on phone calls, etc. I tried having a table and chairs in the booth once for talking to clients and prospects. It really didn't work out as other people just wanted to sit there and rest. In fact, it is easier to talk to people while standing at the booth. Have counter height displays so it is easy to talk while standing.

Another Trade show pet peeve. Eating food in the booth. Again, just say no. You don't want to be eating a sandwich when someone walks up and wants to talk. Eat your food in the food court or outside on a bench during your break.

I like the trade shows that offer attendees food and drink in the expo area. Cocktail parties are a fun way to meet people. Some people think you should not drink while in your booth. That's good idea earlier in the day, wink. I don't have a problem having a glass of wine while talking to a prospect or client who has a beer in his or her hand. Be sure to limit yourself. It could also be a company culture issue decision to drink or not drink at the booth. Be sure everyone is on the same page.

Be sure to leverage the trade show's social media. Include the Twitter handle and hashtag they are using in your own tweets to help promote your booth, your giveaways, your speaking sessions, etc. When setting your goals for the show include some social media impression targets as well.

After The Trade Show

Simple. Follow up and do as you promised. Follow-up with all the leads you received from the trade show. Maybe it's just you that does this. Maybe you have a team. Make sure that everyone you met at the show gets a personal follow-up.

You will now receive the full attendee list from shows that provide this. Add that to your database for future prospect follow-up. Direct mail, phone call follow-up and mailing for next year's show, as well as email if you receive it. Hopefully you are using a good CRM (Customer Relationship Management) software so you can tag these new contacts as people you met at the trade show. Be sure to categorize how hot a sales lead they are. Add the info to campaigns you have set up with your CRM so you can track the budget spent to pipeline and sales created.

Learn from the show. What went well? What needs improvement? Were there other vendors there that you can learn from? Did they have a cool booth, great giveaways, very nice way to hand out literature?

Did you meet fellow exhibitors that could help you sell to more customers? Start a separate database list just for these folks for additional follow-up. Again, good CRM software allows you to categorize this type of information.

If it is a worthwhile show, get more involved next year as a speaker or volunteer.

Use all of this learning for your next trade show to leverage the networking aspects of the show.

Earlier I mentioned that I liked smaller niche trade shows, or conferences. In the Tech industry it can be as specific as a Gartner CIO conference. There are also local Technology Associations. Many of them have events and conferences throughout the year. One of my favorites is the Colorado Technology Association. The best event I have ever attended in all my marketing career is the C-Level @ A Mile High event. I have attended this event as an attendee, a sponsor, and a volunteer, and have done so for 11 years (so far). Here is the blog I wrote about the 2017 event.

Top 10 Reasons to Attend C-Level @ A Mile High 2017

What are you doing on March 16th? I'd like to invite you to attend C-Level @ A Mile High. It is the premier IT event put on by the Colorado Technology Association. I've been in B2B Technology Marketing for much of my career and this is by far the best event I have ever been to as an attendee, a volunteer, and a sponsor. Why? Here are my top 10 reasons:

1. **The Venue** - Sports Authority Field at Mile High. Home of the 3-time **Super Bowl Champions** Denver Broncos! On the Club Level. The picture above is from last year. What a cool place and the view of downtown Denver when the sun sets is amazing.

2. **The Networking** - If you are an IT professional in Colorado (or the region) this is THE event to be at to network with your peers and meet over 60 CIOs and CXOs and learn about the projects they have coming up.

3. **The Celebrities** - There will be over 60 CIOs, CXOs and executive leadership from many of the largest and most

innovative companies in Colorado. They are adding new celebrities each week. So far, companies represented include Arrow Electronics, Intrawest, IQ Navigator, Arcadis, City and County of Denver, Hunter Douglas.

4.   **The Food** - Nobody goes away hungry. This event is a large cocktail party with over 1200 of your closest friends. There are several hour devours stations throughout the Club Level.

5.   **The Silent Auction** - While walking from one Celebrity area to the next, you can check out several stations set up for the silent auction. Last year there were over 89 items from sports paraphernalia, tropical vacations, golf outings, extreme adventures, restaurants, and more.

6.   **The CTA Staff** - The group of dedicated people who run the Colorado Technology Association are incredible. It is amazing what this team does throughout the year.

7.   **The Sponsors** - These companies are very smart as they know a good event to sponsor when they see it. A special thanks to all the sponsors. It is a good group to be associated with, and to learn from.

8.   **Did I Mention The Celebrities?** - Last year the 60 celebrities who participated at this event had over $1 Billion (yes, that's a B) in IT projects. Wouldn't you and your company like to learn more about this year's celebrities?

9.   **The Volunteers** - C-Level @ A Mile High would not happen without the 906 plus volunteer hours that go into making this event a success. Say thank you when you see them.

10.   **It's a Win-Win for You and The Colorado Technology Community.** Check out the recap VIDEO from 2016's event.

Chapter Six – Your Website, and your blog.

If "a picture is worth 1000 words" just think what a web site can be worth.

In my opinion even in today's social media conglomeration of Twitter, Facebook, Instagram, LinkedIn, and Pinterest, your website is extremely important. Hopefully you are using all the marketing tools available to you like social media (the ones that make sense, more on this later) to get people back to your website, learn about your company, and buy/become a customer. You should have content on your website that is important to your client, prospect. A blog on your site is a great way to always have fresh content. The fact that your blog is part of your website is good for SEO, Search Engine Optimization.

Be consistent with your blog. Make sure it is continuously updated. Have you ever gone to someone's blog and the last blog was weeks or months old? If you aren't going to update it consistently don't have one.

Just as you set goals for your business plan and marketing plan, you should set goals for your website. What are you trying to accomplish by having a website? Is it an ecommerce site where you want people to buy products? Are you a services company that relies on your web site to be a "virtual brochure" to get the pertinent information to your prospects so they will want to do business with you?

You can use your website for:

- Webinars
- Articles
- Blogs
- Training
- Promote your staff
- Information about your products.
- Collect information from visitors and add as a lead to your sales pipeline in your CRM
- Talk about how you give back to the community
- Have a sign-up area for your enewsletter
- Promote local, national, international events
- Sign up for white papers and eBooks

Take some time and review competitors' websites as well as web sites of brands you really like or have bought from.

Are the sites static or always changing?

Is there enough information to catch the attention of the prospect? On average you have 8 seconds of time to get someone's attention before they leave your website looking for another.

"A website without any marketing is like having a billboard in your basement."

Make sure that the marketing you do drives people back to your website with a call to action; watch a webinar, download a white paper, etc. Also, make sure you are collecting the data they give you when they sign up. There are several CRM (Customer Relationship Manager) solutions out there for small business; HiRise and salesforce.com are two I am familiar with. Some can automatically enter the information people are adding when signing up directly into your CRM. That makes it very easy to then follow-up with them.

I would recommend working with someone that understands SEO (Search Engine Optimization) when you build or revamp your website. Begin with a "site map" and organize your thoughts as to what you want your site to be. Work with an agency that can help you with these thoughts by talking to you, your customers, and your partners. Even if you work with a freelance website designer do your homework with her/him and make sure they understand the goals of your website. Be sure you also incorporate promoting what social media channels you are on.

Make sure you and your website developer (whether that is in-house or a freelance or with an agency) walk through the following areas:

- Goals of the website
- Design
- Ease of Use
- Copywriting
- Interactivity
- Innovation

- Content

- SEO

- Social Media

Chapter Seven - Digital Media, Online Media, New Media

There are several ways to define marketing via the internet and the latest technologies. In the theme of getting people to your website we will first look at advertising options that are on the web today.

I will go into more detail with some digital or online marketing in separate chapters.

How are you promoting your website? From the website chapter I pointed out a great quote. A website without advertising is like having a billboard in your basement.

Banner Ads

One digital strategy I really don't care for much are banner ads and some ads on websites. I really hate the ones that open up and cover a portion or all of the website. I don't look at the ad; I look for the "close" button. They are so obnoxious I can't believe people are still using them.

A poll by AdweekMedia/Harris states 63% of consumers say they tend to ignore or disregard all Internet ads. The poll also said that among that group, 43% say they don't pay attention to banner ads and 20% ignore search ads. But on the flip side some people do at least look at the ads. So, it would be ok to use some of these if you have the budget and are looking for more brand building opportunities. One of the good things about online ads is you are able to measure their effectiveness through various web analytics tools. Measure and see what's working. Change or stop what's not working.

You can now do extremely targeted ads on LinkedIn and Facebook. This will be discussed in the social media chapter.

Digital Signage, Digital Out of Home (DOOH)
One very interesting thing to me in the "digital space" is digital signage and digital ad networks.

In October of 2009 my family drove to Columbia Missouri for my nieces wedding. Along the way I noticed about 50% of the billboards were giant digital screens.

It turns out there are three significant areas where digital signage is exploding in growth. All of them are in the DOOH (digital out of home) category. The three areas break down into generic advertising where it is the display only, in store retail display to help people make a decision, and extremely interactive touch screen displays people can use to find out information or find a destination.

You are probably exposed to some type of digital signage many times throughout the day; Airports, elevators, fast food restaurants, hotels, health clubs, office building lobby, shopping malls, the list goes on and on.

In fact, according to an Arbitron Digital Place-Based Video Study this type of media reaches over 7 out of 10 U.S. residents each month. The study also reports that more people watch digital place-based video than watch video online, have a Facebook profile or a Smartphone.

PQ Media forecasts that this $6 billion media "industry" will grow 9.4% in the U.S. and 10% globally.

Coca Cola likes this new technology so much it is operating its own network of digital billboards.

ROI is always of interest in advertising and sometimes hard to measure. You can get some information from studies like Arbitron. And the more interactive the digital display is (interactive touch screens) the more data can be collected. It will be interesting to see how ROI is measured as this technology grows and defines itself more and more. It will also be fun to watch how creative the advertising becomes.

Digital signage may or may not be a part of your marketing plan but it is certainly a cool thing to think about.

QR Codes

Another interesting use of digital marketing are QR Codes or 2D Bar Codes. The QR Code is a two-dimensional code read by a bar code reader. These readers are in cell phones with cameras. The QR Code image is usually a square with different black rectangular images. When you have the correct software on your camera phone you hover over the image and it gives you details. That can be a link to a micro site, a quick video, or other creative ways to use mobile technology for marketing. It is also an innovative way to connect traditional media (a magazine ad or poster at a trade show) with digital media (a QR code that takes you to a video of the product).

This technology is fairly inexpensive to implement.

Chapter Eight - Websites and Search Engine Optimization

How can you leverage one of the most cost-effective ways to get people to your website? Search Engine Optimization. The cool thing about search is that people are looking for you and your products. They are searching for products and information on Google and Bing.

There are two areas to review with SEO.

Optimizing your website for PPC (Pay Per Click) and campaigns around Organic or free searches. In an earlier chapter we talked about making sure when you design your website you talk with someone about SEO. This will help make sure your site is search friendly for the "spiders" that the Googles of the world use to crawl through the World Wide Web in search of the name or phrase (key words) people are typing in when searching for a product or service while indexing the sites.

We'll start with "meta tags" – When looking at any website go to the "View" menu option in your browser. Click on it and there will be a "source" or "view source" option to choose. Select that one and it will bring up a page full of code. This code represents the language put in when the site was developed. It includes the meta name of the site, as well as meta tag key words. All very important for search engines. Work with your website designer on learning where to add this information and be able to update it on your own as well. Make sure that when your website is done you are comfortable in updating information and making changes so you don't need to rely on the developer for every change.

This area is important as well for keywords and our next topic; PPC or Pay Per Click campaigns.

First, we will talk about getting your ranking high in search based on "organic" or free searches.

Look up a product or service you are interested in on Google. You will see some results on the top and on the right-hand side that say "ads". Those are the ads that you can buy as part of your pay per click campaign. More on that later. In some instances, there are areas right below the top that are some type of sponsored list, and below that are the free listings.

To get these free or organic search results you need to again optimize your site for key words as well as do some type of link building activity. What that means is have your website mentioned and the actual URL (uniform resource locator), your website address in the site. In many searches there is a listing for Wikipedia. Helpful hint: Is there a Wikipedia site about your company? If yes, good for you. If not, start one. But be sure to manage it as anyone can add information to it.

When you create your link building campaign you need to think of partnerships that would help your site get better organic search results. Are you a member of a chamber of commerce? Do they list their members with hot links back to their website? How about industry trade associations? Did you get an article written in a local magazine or newspaper? Usually they have online version as well that will have a link. If you attend industry trade shows the fact that you have a booth may give you a link. Look for other sponsorship opportunities with the shows you attend as there may be other opportunities to get your website link on other websites. The more websites that are talking about you and your product with links back to your site, the better your organic search results will be.

You can also start a "partner" page on your site with links back to their sites like the ones we noted above; chambers of commerce, industry trade information. Be sure to also have a "Press" area on your website. This is where you can list the articles you have been mentioned in with links back to them, as well as a list of press releases. Warning: if you do this please keep it current. You don't want people coming to your site and the information is old. Keep the old but make sure there are plenty of new listings as well.

Including Social Media in your marketing campaigns will also help SEO. The more you tweet and post about your product with links back to your site, the more this will help with your ranking as people come to your site from clicking the links.

Pay Per Click

Pay per click (PPC) is where you actually are paying Google and Bing every time someone clicks on your ad during a search.

Earlier I noted how after a search there are ads on the top of the page as well as the right-hand side of the page.

The only time you get charged for those ads is when someone clicks on the ad. Google analytics helps you track to see how many people are clicking on the ads. Google AdWords helps you get set up with correct keywords to have the ad show up. You can manage your budget and pay just what you want. It can also be a daunting process to not keep spending more and more.

Some people think having the ads on the page next to an organic search result increases your chances of someone clicking on the ad. Others feel the ads are ignored and people only look at the organic searches. As I mentioned in the previous chapter a poll by AdweekMedia/Harris some 63% of consumers say they tend to ignore or disregard all Internet ads. So be sure to watch your results.

The nice thing about these ad programs is you can budget how much you spend. You may be inclined to continue to increase your ad budget but again, try to measure as much of this as possible to see if you are getting the results you desire.

To learn more about this On Google click on "Advertising programs" and in Bing "advertise" on each home page. I worked for a startup business and learned search engine optimization after reading a couple books (Winning Results With Google AdWords by Andrew Goodman, and Search Engine Visibility by Shari Thurow) and learned about AdWords from all the help and tips that Google provides. The startup went from nowhere on the results pages to rankings 1, 2 and 3 spots in the free organic search results.

There is an industry around this with consultants and entire companies that help businesses with SEO consulting so there is a vast amount of help out there if you need it. There are many websites and books as well. It is a decision of if you have the staff to do it yourself, or hire a consultant. If you already work with an agency they may be able to help you as well. I mentioned there are also various ways to measure including Google analytics. You can also integrate with CRMs like a salesforce.com to actually track click to purchase. Good luck.

Chapter Nine - Email Marketing

Another extremely great way to keep in contact with your current customers and prospects is through permission-based email marketing.

This chapter is not about sending your customers common email using your ordinary email application. Boring! Not only boring but most Internet Service Providers (ISPs) in their attempt to eliminate or reduce junk mail, are making it harder and harder for you to send emails to more than one person at a time. This chapter is about how integrated email marketing publications can promote you and your business's personality, build customer loyalty, and reach new customers.

How much money do you spend on marketing? How much time do you take marketing to new prospects versus existing clients? How much time would you like to spend on marketing? And how much money would you like to spend? Or should I ask how much time and money would you like to save?

Let's consider some of the benefits of email newsletters.

Email newsletters save money. When you put a direct mail campaign together (postcard, letter, hard copy newsletter, etc.) you have several costs involved. The cost of creating the marketing piece, employee time, your time or cost for an agency to do it, the production cost of the direct mail piece itself, as well as the cost of postage. A recent study by McKinsey and Company shows the average cost for direct mail is $2.00 per direct mail piece versus 3 to 10 cents per email.

Wouldn't it be nice to have a cost savings like that? You could invest it back into your business for equipment, personnel, or the bank for the next rainy day.

Email newsletters get results. When you send a direct mail piece (such as a postcard, a letter) what kind of response do you get? How many postcards or letters did you send? Jupiter Communications reports that the average response rate for direct mail is 1-2% (that's generous in my opinion). Compare that to typical email marketing response rates of 15% - even higher if you have good email lists (loyal customers)!

Hmm, let's see, a 15% response rate for email marketing that costs on average 3 to 10 cents per message, compared to a 1-2% response rate for direct mail that costs $2.00 per message.

You can see, immediately, the effectiveness of your email newsletters. The better services provide this. When you deliver a postcard or direct mail piece, do you know when it's thrown in the trash? What sections of your brochure or hard copy newsletter are read? How do you gauge how your overall marketing campaign is doing? The best email marketing and publishing services provide detailed reporting. You can track how many emails were sent, how many people actually opened your messages, how many bad email addresses you have, how many unsubscribed, how many read specific portions of your newsletter. It's great, because you can review these reports and see who's reading your article, your new employee's bio, your recipe. Using this information allows you to produce an even better email newsletter next month. And if done properly you can then categorize the people who clicked though on certain areas of your newsletter and do follow-up email marketing just to them. Categorize and send a reminder email for a seminar they signed up for. You can also send more information on a product they clicked on.

Email newsletters increases customer loyalty - not satisfaction, loyalty. When you get email from a company whose product or services you appreciate, do you subsequently do more or less business with them? If the email is well written, and its call-to-action clear, you're probably going to be a return customer. On-going client communication is essential for building customer loyalty. According to Midnet Media, frequent permission-based email newsletters reduce customer attrition. You will be able to keep clients informed about what's happening at your business, about new employees, special events, and special sales. Midnet Media also reports that regular email marketing to existing customers generates a 15-50% increase in total business.

Once you have sent one or two of these custom designed email newsletters, your customers will know that it is useful and informative information from a person they trust. Then that "send to a friend" feature you've added to your email newsletter will really come in handy and you can watch your client list grow and grow... in a very cost effective, permission-based way.

A comment about "send to a fiend" studies show they aren't used that much and most people just forward using their email system. A much better way these days is to add "share" buttons throughout your enewsletter. That way people can click on that and share with all their friends on Facebook, or send to all their contacts on Twitter or LinkedIn. Cool huh?

Good luck to you and your business. Save a tree, send email newsletters!

In the appendix of this book look for additional information including "10 Tips For Successful Email Marketing".

Chapter Ten - Social Media and Social Selling

Unless you have been sleeping under a rock the last few years, you have watched in amazement the explosion of social media. It started out with MySpace being the main social site but that has since been dwarfed by Facebook, Twitter, LinkedIn, Instagram and Pinterest.

The numbers are astonishing, according to Facebook statistics as of the second quarter of 2018, Facebook had 2.23 billion monthly active users.

There are 336 million Twitter users, 500 million registered LinkedIn users, and 400 million Instagram users.

An AP-CNBC poll found that 57% of Facebook users said they never click on ads or other sponsored content when they use the site. Another 26% said they hardly ever engage in such activity. Only 4% of users say they often click on ads. They said these results are only slightly better than the 2-3 percent click through rate some experts consider the benchmark for effective banner ads.

It is interesting that Google is so successful because people go there to click on ads and search results when looking for something.

There are several other social sites out there like Pinterest. All have their niche followers. I'll focus mostly on Facebook, LinkedIn and Twitter and how these might help you with marketing and most importantly word of mouth (Like).

Facebook is absolutely amazing for advertisers (in that you can customize who will see your ads), but as mentioned earlier is anyone noticing the ads? It's fun to add what you like in Facebook. I don't give too much personal info though.

One day I was on Facebook and there was an ad in the side for Legos. I realized that since I had "liked" the Lego page Lego can now search for people who like them and have their ad show up on those pages.

True, it's really fascinating with an "ooh that's kind of creepy" aspect at the same time. Go ahead and research the ads within Facebook. You can literally drill down and look for people who are CMO's in Denver. Then the ads you run will only show up on their pages. Talk about targeted marketing. Facebook may be a place where people want to communicate with friends and not be bothered with ads. Just like all advertising online it is measurable. You will be able to measure fairly quickly and easily how effective your ads are, if you should add or change or take them off.

Ads aside, Facebook may be a great place for you to have a page for your business, and then get people to sign up as fans, likes, whatever the term will be when you read this.

Just like a website and a blog as we discussed earlier in the book, if you decide to do this it is a full-time job. People are looking at these sites every day. An update once a month or once a week isn't going to cut it. If you engage your fans who have signed up for your Facebook page it could be much more successful than ads. Especially when they like and share with their friends.

Social media in my opinion is the closest thing to true word of mouth. I'm not talking about a funny video about a baby that goes viral and everyone watches it and shares it with their friends. I bet in most cases if you ask what that funny video was trying to sell, people couldn't answer. Was that for car insurance? Investment advisors? Diapers?

Social media sites like Facebook can really turn into the water cooler or neighborhood fence where people gather and talk about the latest news, and share ideas when someone is looking for a good computer. If you are on Facebook you have probably seen where sometimes your postings go unnoticed, and others several people comment. Those people are usually spread out across the country. I like to call Facebook the virtual water cooler. Again, even though people are spread out, the information, the feeling, is local. I have seen some companies do Facebook well, like Dell computer and Cascadian Farms.

I spoke earlier about how it is good to write an article for a local paper. I also take advantage of the blog capabilities on LinkedIn. Here is my first blog post:

10 Tips for Leveraging Twitter and LinkedIn

Greetings, a subtitle to this blog could be "Hey Twitter, what's up with @ and #?"

85% of B2B buyers use social media during the buying process. - ITSMA/CFO magazine.

Here are some thoughts around social media and how you can leverage Twitter and LinkedIn to help amplify the messages around your company's great content and events and help you with your social selling. Remember, listen first and interact. Don't spam.

Tip #1. **Think of Twitter as a search engine**. Because it is. Search VMUG in your Twitter page. You will see endless tweets about local VMUGs, VMUG leaders, upcoming VMUG User Conferences and Forums, etc. As seen in the above picture from VMworld 2014, **VMware** has a strong community both offline and online. Seth Godin would affectionately call this a tribe. VMUG, VMware's user group community, now has 100,000 members. Follow the VMUGs and VMUG leaders and join in the conversation. If you are part of this tribe be sure to follow @MyVMUG .

Tip #2 @ is an address (a twitter handle). My address is @JohndMeyer. When you include these addresses, and from Tip #1 @MyVMUG, the followers of those Twitter handles can see what you tweeted. If you start your tweet with a Twitter handle it is a message that goes directly to that person.

Tip #3 # (hashtag) represents a keyword for a topic. I could say "I am looking forward to the #VMUG event in Minneapolis". # also measures "trends" in conversations.

Tip #4 Get More Specific. Say "See you at Minneapolis #VMUG event @vmrick @rcvmug @mnvmug" Rick Schlander @vmrick is MN VMUG leader.

Tip #5 Don't overdo @ or # in any one tweet. You have 280 characters to get your point across. Spaces are included in that count. Keep to 200 characters for re-tweeting. Begin your message with RT and it will prompt people to re-tweet your message. It works! Try it. You need room for their twitter handle as well and that is why they recommend 200 characters for re-tweeting.

Tip #6 Amplify! Pictures add interest. Be active and re-tweet messages from key influencers you are following. That will help them follow you as well. Favorite their messages. And reply to them and tell them why you liked the message. A picture paints 1000 words, and it grabs people's attention. Add photos of the event you are attending, etc.

Tip #7 Follow Influencers at your Strategic Partners. Nobody cares what you had for breakfast but they do care that a CEO from your partner tweeted out a new strategic relationship with your company.

Tip #8 Mix it up and Be Consistent. Be sure to tweet about personal interests as well as business, add some famous quotes, and include info on any sports you follow. Also, be consistent with your social media activities. Some say early morning and late afternoon are most active on social media. I usually post a few things in the morning and late afternoon. And maybe a few at lunch time. After you do it for a while it will become part of your routine, just as the times you have set aside for core email.

Tip #9 Feeling Overwhelmed? Two helpful tools with LinkedIn and HootSuite. **LinkedIn** allows you to post to Twitter at the same time. Keep in mind that you have a lot of character room in LinkedIn. 280 characters with Twitter. **HootSuite** is a great tool for scheduling tweets, posts and doing analytics around what is trending.

Tip #10 Maximize Your LinkedIn profile. Follow the LinkedIn suggestions to get to 100%, Use a Professional photo, have a link to your company in your profile, add "keywords" to your profile, build your network and **personalize** your requests. Join influential LinkedIn Groups and participate. Connect with the Group owners as well.

Remember: What happens on the internet stays on the internet. Be positive and professional.

1. Bonus: There are a gazillion articles online to help your social selling. Really. Just Google it. Here is a good article from **Inc**. 6 Tips For Using Social Media to Boost Sales. Enjoy!

LinkedIn is especially powerful for B2B.

5 Reasons Why LinkedIn ROCKS B2B

1. LinkedIn Groups- Where else can you network online with the same people you are able to network with in person? And with more than 280 characters. You may be a member of a large industry group that has annual conferences. There are also groups that share similar interests, as well as local community groups. In my blog I included a picture from an annual event that the Colorado Technology Association puts on, the APEX awards. So not only can you network in person, CTA has a LinkedIn Group with daily conversations on what is happening in the community.

2. LinkedIn's biggest secret - Open and click through rates of the LinkedIn Group Opt In email digests. These go out to their 300,000,000 members. If you are like me, you are a member of several groups. Right now, maximum number you are allowed to join is 50. Some groups have 1000 members, some have over 100,000 members. I would imagine this LinkedIn group email platform could be the biggest opt in email list(s) in the history of email. It will be interesting to see how and if LinkedIn leverages this asset in the future.

3. Your Online Rolodex - LinkedIn is a fantastic way to stay in touch with your network, and build it. When I get business cards I look the person up on LinkedIn, write a personal message to connect on LinkedIn, and throw the business card away. All the info I need is on LinkedIn. Wherever the person moves to we will be connected. That same relationship network can help you with warm introductions to people you would like to meet and network with.

The three above are free. You of course can pay a minimal fee for Premier/Business for additional benefits. The two below have a cost related but may be perfect for your business goals and objectives. By the way, they are also the two biggest areas of growth for LinkedIn.

4. LinkedIn Marketing - If you want to learn about leveraging Big Data for valuable analytics, you need look any further than the power of advertising on social media. You can target your precious marketing dollars to the people that may be most interested in your solutions. No more spray and pray. If you want to reach out to CXOs most interested in earth moving equipment, cancer research, medical devices, or video surveillance technologies, you can. And with "Influencers" and "Pulse", LinkedIn is becoming *the* content hub for Subject Matter Experts.

5. LinkedIn Sales - LinkedIn encapsulates all the items above to really help sales professionals as well as their entire team do a better job of researching companies, the people they would like to network with, and allows for warm introductions. At a basic level the people you are connected with may be connected to the person you want to talk to who is also a member of the LinkedIn group you or your mutual prospect is a member of. With the millions of business professionals on LinkedIn, this is a valuable resource.

In the spirit of All Marketing Is Local, Social Selling is a key ingredient to your marketing mix. You can leverage social media channels to help you reach new customers.

Seven Tips for Social Selling Success (Part 1)

How are your sales numbers? Are you finding the following statistics happening more than ever?

Customers often complete 57% of their due diligence on a solution before engaging with a supplier. – CEB

85% of B2B buyers use social media during the buying process. - ITSMA/CFO magazine.

However, the most successful sales professionals are still setting meetings during this time. How? You may have seen some blogs and articles about Social Selling. Why is it so important to engage on social media? Here is an interesting result from a study that the **Challenger team** conducted with over 1,000 sales professionals:

"The single most powerful behavior separating high performers from core performers is using social media as a critical channel to engage customers and generate leads." - The Challenger Customer

Here are some tips you can use to get involved in social selling:

1. **Set a goal and a strategy**. This isn't about spamming people. This is about building your credibility online through thought leadership. You want the influencers (Mobilizers if you are studying the Challenger Customer) you'd like to talk to in accounts to see you as a SME (Subject Matter Expert) and thought leader.

2. **How do you get there? Start by seeing what your Social Selling Index (SSI) score is**. You are on LinkedIn so you should check it out online. This week my score is 89. SSI scores fluctuate week to week based on influence. It is a performance metric as a social seller. You can also see how you rank within your industry as well as the overall LinkedIn

network. Also, do not think of your LinkedIn profile as a resume, it is your personal brand. Think of that as you update your profile.

3.   **Make a goal to improve your SSI scor**e. LinkedIn ranks your score based on four elements of social selling: **Establish** your professional brand - **Find** the right people - **Engage** with insights - and **Build** relationships. LinkedIn provides you with several tips to improve in all four areas. You should also upgrade to the LinkedIn premium version if you aren't already. It provides more information that you would be looking for as a social seller. And if your company is serious about social selling you should have your team look into Sales Navigator.

4.   **Listen**. Review your goals and strategy from tip one. Decide who the influencers/mobilizers are in the accounts you are targeting and see where they are active. If they post something of interest on LinkedIn "like" it. If they post something interesting on Twitter re-tweet it. Follow them as well. Do you have mutual connections on their LinkedIn profiles? Are you a member of the same LinkedIn groups?

5. **Share**. To help build your credibility (tip 1) be proactive with sharing pertinent content to your LinkedIn followers. It could be an interesting article about your industry, an industry executive receiving an award, etc. Add comments to the conversation on pertinent discussions in groups you are a member of that are strong in your industry. You can also write a blog on LinkedIn Pulse. If you are not comfortable with that, yet, you can write an introductory paragraph to a blog from one of your company's thought leaders and share a link to the blog. Be sure to use pictures and graphics. That adds a lot for attention.

6. **Challenge yourself**. Just as you are challenging your customers and prospects with thought provoking information, challenge yourself as well to be an even stronger social seller. Social selling is good for sharing information you think your customers and prospects should look at for their purchase research and decisions. Are you comfortable on LinkedIn but not Twitter? Then you should set up a Twitter account, or go back to the one you started way back when and start engaging. I will review this more in part 2 of this blog. In the meantime, you can review 10 Tips

<u>for Leveraging LinkedIn and Twitter</u>. You will be surprised how many of your customers and prospects are on Twitter. You will also see how many user communities in your industry are active there. Industry influencers and thought leaders that your prospects and customers follow are also very active on Twitter.

7.   **Listen, Share, Connect.** I will have more tactical ideas in part 2 of this blog. For now, think strategically. Set your goals, improve your social selling index, listen to your customers and prospects. Start sharing like the thought leader and subject matter expert you are. Challenge yourself, continually. Soon you will be comfortable and reaching out directly with an InMail, or a request to connect, an introduction from a mutual connection, and soon after a meeting.

You should also check in with your company's social media team. Ask what resources are available like a blog community, amplification and analysis tools, and most importantly social media guidelines.

Good luck and good social selling.

Seven Tips For Social Selling Success (Part 2)

In the first blog we reviewed the importance of engaging on social media since so many customers and prospects are utilizing social media when they research information on solutions they are looking for. We also reviewed the importance of listening first, and then engaging.

By now you have set your goals, reviewed your social selling index (SSI), and have started listening to your customers and prospects.

Now let's review some ideas on how to build your presence on social media, and engage with your customers and prospects. As we pointed out in Part 1: *Listen, Engage, Connect*.

1.   **Continue to build your presence online**. Join and engage with pertinent groups on LinkedIn. What groups are the influencers, mobilizers, at your prospects and customers

members of? Comment and follow some of the discussions where you can add some value with your thought leadership. Start a discussion. Write a blog on LinkedIn Pulse. Review the tips on how to improve your SSI from part 1 of this blog.

2. **Review and join communities on Twitter**. Many of the user communities in your industry will have their own Twitter handle. When you view the particular Twitter handle there should be "Lists" to the right of Tweets, Following, Followers, Likes. Review their lists. Click on the List that seems most relevant or interesting. In the upper left you will see "Members". Click on that and follow all the members. Engage by retweeting some of their tweets. It is a great way to get involved with the thought leaders in your industry. Many of them will follow you back.

3. **Connect and engage with your brand enthusiasts**. These can be your fellow employees, subject matter experts and bloggers in your company, as well as influencers and analysts in your industry that follow your company and may participate at events. You should also follow key customers, as well as the partners you work with that help sell and

support your solutions. You can see that you can be part of quite a large ecosystem.

4. **Utilize social media scheduling tools like Hootsuite, Sprout Social, and Buffer.** There are many solutions out there that can help you manage your time and schedule posts throughout the week. Remember to mix it up. Share professional interests, business interests, as well as personal interests. Follow pertinent online magazines and blogs and share that content as well.

5. **Engage and connect with your customers and prospects**. By now you have built a stronger presence online and have built credibility with your thought leadership. You've listened to what your customers and prospects are saying, and may have an understanding on where they are at with their buyers' journey. Help them with that journey by sharing points of view that are valuable to them. If you are not connected you can also send an InMail on LinkedIn or have a mutual connection make an introduction.

6. **Review Analytics Tools to see how you are doing**. You have already used LinkedIn to see what your Social

Selling Index is. You can also use Twitter, Hootsuite, Sprout Social, Buffer and other tools to measure your engagement with your tweets and posts. They are a great way to see the engagement level of your tweets. Retweets, impressions, mentions, follower engagement, etc. You can see if there are any thought leadership posts worth sharing again. Most of these tools have a free version, as well as more robust solutions with a cost.

7. **Additional Marketing Automation and Measurement Tools**. There are many other solutions out there now that can help sales and marketing teams work together on social selling plans. As sales teams refine their lists of accounts they are targeting you can utilize ABM (Account Based Marketing) as a way to strategically and tactically plan to reach out and educate your prospects and customers. With all the tools available now to measure activity online, the data that is gathered can be extremely helpful. If you followed Dreamforce at all last week you heard about Einstein and how that can also help with social selling. That is just one of the many solutions out there that can help you be more successful.

Good luck with getting more comfortable with social media and utilizing these tips to help you with social selling.

It is an exciting time for sales and marketing teams to work closely together and leverage the solutions available to them to help you exceed your goals.

Good social selling.

Account Based Marketing and Social Selling. A B2B Marketers Dream Come True.

Recently I read Alexander Hamilton by Ron Chernow. I highly recommend it. I had no idea how much Hamilton was involved in forming our government, our military, our banking and financial system. In my blog I added a picture of New York City. It is the center of the financial world in large part due to Hamilton. When he lived there the population was 85,000. It is now 14 million.

It is a big city with many, many companies. A bit daunting if you are a sales executive and have that as your territory. Or maybe not if you implement an Account Based Marketing strategy. By the way, I think Hamilton would have loved the Internet and all the technology we have at our fingertips today.

Let's begin. Many of us have been doing "Account Based Marketing" for years. Recently it has gotten more interesting and fun due to the cool technology we can use to implement, manage, and measure it.

The key areas of Account Based Marketing include:

- **Marketing and sales meet as a team to define what Account Based Marketing is and to develop a mutually agreed upon plan**. Create a SLA (Service Level Agreement) so everyone knows which team members are in charge of what areas and can report back when it is time for the ongoing measurement of the campaign. This will help define what success looks like and what to measure along the way. Create a dashboard of KPI metrics for presentations and review with the various sales leaders and managers.

- **Developing the list of accounts to work with.** Look at additional information and predictive analytics on accounts to see which may be the right ones to target. This could be based on initial tracking with sales, existing accounts where you want to grow new business, targeted competitors accounts, strategic new logos. All this can be part of the process for an account scoring model to help decide which accounts should be included in the campaign. During this stage you can also define the personas of who you will be reaching out to. Who are the key influencers and decisions makers? If you are a Challenger Customer student, who is the mobilizer?

- **Create/leverage content and develop the ABM Campaign**. I mentioned earlier how the technology we have now makes ABM even more exciting. One of these areas is with Real Time Personalization when prospects and customers visit your website. As you build out your plan of both online and offline activities, you can incorporate activity on your website that becomes personalized based on who visits. A visitor who has previously downloaded a whitepaper may come back and see an announcement of a webinar that ties in with the info from the white paper. Someone else who has downloaded the white paper and watched the webinar may see an announcement for a local event in their area. These announcements are not pop up ads. Those are horrible. Make it a part of the website, like a navigation sidebar, so you can integrate your content in an appealing way. That could also tie in to a personal phone call from the sales rep inviting them to the same event. All of this would be part of the integrated project plan that includes email, direct mail, webinars, online ads, local events, industry trade shows, etc.

- **Include Social Selling into the ABM plan**. Measuring online activity can be increased even more with social media and social selling. Marketing and sales have previously agreed on the accounts you are including in the ABM campaign. You may also incorporate setting up streams in your teams, and sales reps, Hootsuite (or other social media scheduling tools) to follow the accounts Twitter handle, as well as key stakeholders within those accounts that have Twitter handles. The blending of online activity (web visits, SEO Pay Per Clicks, online ad clicks), offline events, and social selling will increase the likelihood of sales engagement with the prospects and customers. If you would like additional help on Social Selling read Seven Tips for Social Selling Success **Part 1** and **Part 2**.

- **Measure, review, and improve**. During the campaign you will be meeting in previously decided on meetings with the sales team to see how the campaign is going and what areas could be improved. The reports you put together can be various dashboards. An executive overview for the sales leadership, and more detailed drill down for the sales managers working with the accounts. Some of this can be done with the CRM and marketing automation tools you use, or predefined templates and a simple spreadsheet. Measure everything within the campaign so you can track the KPIs you are interested in and of course ROI.

When you incorporate an Account Based Marketing plan into your marketing and sales strategy you will see a huge difference. No more spraying and praying! Now the size of New York City does not look as daunting. You can target smartly and see your success rate soar. And if you can make it there...

Good Marketing and Selling!

Chapter Eleven - Word of Mouth

This is the Holy Grail – this is what will really grow your business, retain clients, and bring in new customers. This applies whether you are a small business with a local community following or one with national or international clients. As a reminder, in order to have positive word of mouth, you must first have a fantastic product, business, and employees that people are going to want to talk about.

We've been talking a lot about positive word of mouth. Let's check in with another reality; Negative word of mouth. Negative word of mouth can spread like wildfire. But, if you are doing everything right for every disgruntled client you probably have 10 other happy clients. Customer service people don't get calls from happy customers when things are going right. They get calls when someone is upset because something is broken, or not going right. If that person doesn't get a satisfactory answer, he or she will let everyone know about it. That's one of the negative things about social media. It makes it even easier to spread that wild fire of negative opinion.

On the flip side, social media also makes it easy to put those fires out as well as spread good news. Be up front if someone is irritated. Try to fix it. And respond to it quickly online. You should be proactive if something goes wrong that will affect your clients. Let them here it from you first if at all possible and what you are doing about it to fix the problem. Send an email newsletter update, post it on your social media pages, and then follow-up the same when the problem is resolved.

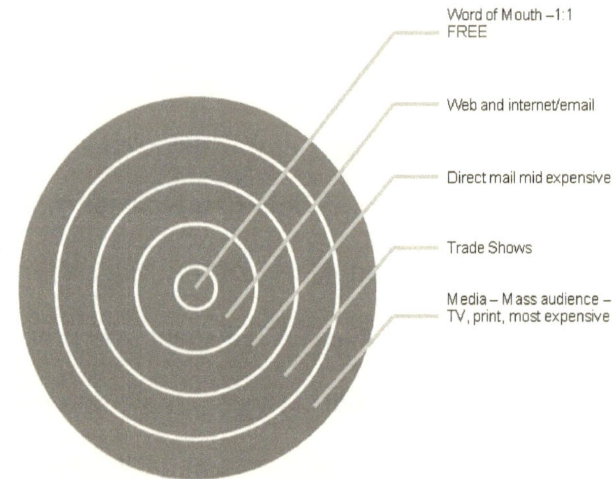

Cost of Influence

With word of mouth, we have finally gotten to the bullseye center of the dart board. The free part of the dart board. You have probably been in a situation where you needed something repaired in your house. If you are like me, you ask a trusted neighbor who he or she uses to maintain their boiler, or who did Mike use for his new roof? That is true word of mouth. Mike has had success with a vendor and is happy with his guy, so he recommends that person. As humans, we'd much rather go with someone we trust versus doing all the research to try to find that vendor.

This type of conversation can happen in a casual discussion over the fence, at the water cooler, or maybe a phone call. As a business owner, or head of marketing and communications, maybe you are both. It is up to you to nurture the relationship so that you get these types of referrals. Again, local marketing. You may even get a complimentary mention on your Facebook page.

It's also up to you to leverage the different marketing tools I've talked about to keep information in front of your clients. Another one of my favorite books is "Word of Mouth Marketing" by Andy Sernovitz. Andy writes "Word of mouth is lazy. You've got to help it along if you expect it to go anywhere. You need a super-simple message and help people share it."

You should also not be afraid to ask your happy clients if they would be a referral for other potential clients, and if you can use a testimonial in your marketing material. Have customer testimonials on your website and literature. In your next email newsletter ask people to forward it to a friend, someone they think might enjoy your service. Have share buttons in the email so people can easily click the share to have their Facebook friends see who they like.

As we discussed earlier, you may not be able to afford TV or radio ads, but you can look into events large media organizations have that you could leverage to get your name out there like "The best of town" article. Become a writer yourself in a local paper or magazine.

Water Cooler and the Neighborhood Fence.

When I first thought of writing this book, I envisioned the cover graphic to be a 1950's style look with two neighbors talking at their mutual waste high fence. Each holding a blackberry or iPhone. The explosion of digital technology has really empowered the aspect of local marketing, word of mouth.

The same can be said for the water cooler at the office. As I said earlier, to me social media is the new digital water cooler, as well as the neighborhood fence that really helps spread local word of mouth marketing.

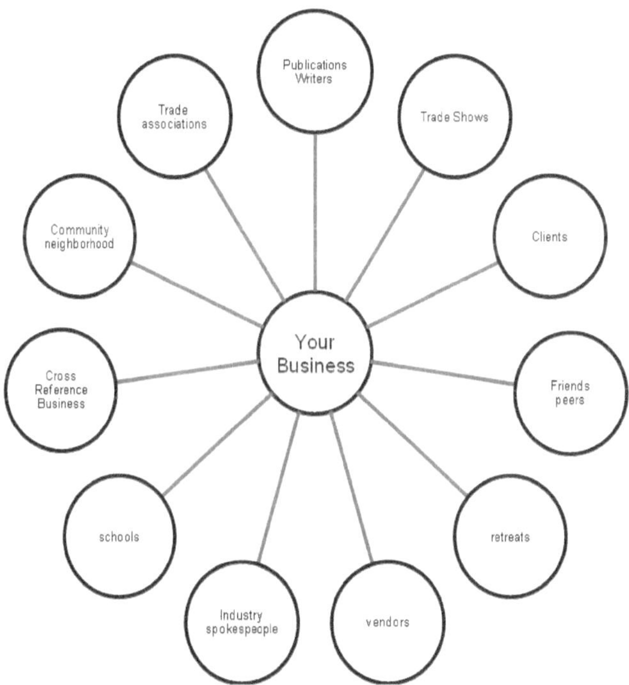

Your Company's Sphere of Influence

When you are reviewing your marketing plan, build a Sphere of Influence like this. You may have more people or organizations you can reach out to, network with, to help build your word of mouth.

Then review the marketing dart board and think of ways you can leverage marketing tools to help your word of mouth grow with all your "local" ideas.

How can you leverage the traditional media to write a story about what you do? Did you know that over 50% of the stories you read in newspapers and magazines were started from a PR outreach? That would include information from a press release or a strategic outreach as part of an overall communications plan. How can you do that? How can you get into that action? Just as you should know your audience, know where your audience goes to get information. Build relationships with writers in those publications, and also see if you can become a writer in those publications.

At the beginning of the book I asked you to write down your favorite restaurant. Think of that restaurant now. Why is it your favorite? How many people have you recommended it to? Did you like its Facebook page? Share the page with your friends? Word of mouth is powerful isn't it?

As Steve Jobs used to say at every conference. One more thing:

5 Reasons Why All Marketing Is Local

The Holy Grail of marketing is Word of Mouth. What are ways to nurture the relationships you have to get existing loyal customers to introduce you to new prospects, and how do you get into the Sphere of Influence that these prospects go to in order to gather information to help them in their personal buyer's journey? Full discloser: I worked for Hitachi Data Systems and some of these examples are examples of the activity we did with our strategic partner VMware.

1. Industry Trade Shows – An event we co-sponsored with them was the VMworld conference in San Francisco. Leverage activities involved within industry trade shows. In this case we were able to leverage private rooms for meetings with customers and prospects that were attending. We also invited customers, and partners within VMware and their user group VMUG, to bring prospects to our booth to speak with subject matter experts.

2. Email - Email is not dead. Big Data Analytics has made it stronger than ever. Today there are so many ways to track people through the buyer's journey. It is getting much easier to invite the right people to the right event at the right time. We are doing more of this and have seen open rates to invites for upcoming events grow from 8% open rate to over 40%.

3. LinkedIn - What? How can a social media platform with over 350 million members be local? Think Sphere of Influence. Think LinkedIn groups. Looking at the Industry Trade show example above, there are VMware related groups with a virtual group, as well as a partner group. These bring together like minded people within a local sphere of influence for discussions and networking.

4. Twitter - Excuse me? With close to 300 million people tweeting all day how can that be local? Again, think sphere of influence, and in this case "lists". Look at one of your favorite twitter handles, think B2B industry specific, and see if it has lists.

I mentioned VMware earlier. Their VMUG user group community has a strong twitter handle. It has three very influential lists; Leaders, Board of Directors, and Local VMUGs. Talk about local marketing!

5. Local Trade Associations - These could be your local chambers of commerce. I work in high tech and we are members of several local technology associations and tech councils. Talk about sphere of influence. Think about what local associations your target audience may be a member of. This is where they go to network with their peers and learn about what's new. Join these associations and become an active member. It is fun.

It is all about figuring out what aspects of a prospects' sphere of influence you can get involved with. Nurture ways to engage and build trusted and loyal relationships. Some people call this target marketing, I call it local marketing. My favorite marketing writer, Seth Godin, calls it micro market. He wrote a blog about it called "Mass production and mass media". Google it.

Influencer Marketing and Word of Mouth.

What exactly is Influencer Marketing? The Wikipedia definition says this about that: **Influencer marketing** (also **influence marketing**) is a form of **marketing** in which focus is placed on influential people rather than the target **market** as a whole. It identifies the individuals that have **influence** over potential buyers, and orients **marketing** activities around these **influencers**.

In a recent Forbes article "Why Influencer marketing will explode in 2017" writer AJ Agrawal said to call it "influencer marketing" is really only the beginning. What's truly happening is a broader shift, as more and more people are discovering the art of personal branding.

When you have a personal brand, when you have an audience and people see you as a ***thought leader*** in your specific niche or market, you have something no one else does: you have people's attention."

The brand can be personal or company brand. That is the goal. When you and or your company are seen as the thought leader in your industry, your niche, that is when Influencer Marketing (also known as word of mouth) really does explode.

How does that happen? Well, to quote Seth Godin, first you have to have an amazing product and company. And when you do, what are the ways to help promote that through word of mouth and Influencer Marketing? I believe the two smartest areas to focus are customer conferences and social media.

Does "Insanely Great" ring a bell? Or "there is one more thing"? Both could be heard from Steve Jobs at Apple conferences. Talk about a trusted brand, both personal and company. I recently was reminded of this at Okta's Oktane17. (Full disclosure I worked at Okta). Okta has amazing customer loyalty. It is impressive looking at all their customer testimonials on their website. What was better than that was to be in the middle of the 2,000 attendees at the end of August at this conference. The attendees were customers, prospects, and writers/bloggers in the industry. Beautiful. You see the same type of loyalty and influencer or peer to peer conversations, (word of mouth) at other conferences like Dreamforce.

Add social media to the mix and you do get that Influencer explosion. Writers and bloggers at the conference sending out tweets and blog posts about the conference, the speakers, the announcements. The customers and employees amplifying those messages through retweets and shares. All this boils down to my favorite type of marketing "Word of Mouth" as I point out in this book. I really do believe smart marketers have been doing "Influencer Marketing" for years through word of mouth and finding the Influencers to truthfully talk about your brand.

What is a blog without some statistics about the subject? Search Engine Watch has Six Stats on the Importance of Trust in Influencer Marketing. One that most marketers are well aware of **"83% of consumers trust recommendations from their peers over advertising**." (Nielsen)

So, what are you doing to build your brand through Influencer marketing? How are you accelerating the word of mouth that is happening about your insanely great product/company? Find your influencers and nurture them at customer conferences and social media. See what happens.

Follow me on Twitter to see what else I am thinking about in marketing, technology and just plain fun topics. @JohndMeyer

Appendix:

Some final thoughts and ideas for you:

Ten Tips for Successful Email Marketing

1. Let your clients know your email newsletter is from you. Your company name (your brand) should be in the subject line. You have very loyal customers with very busy inboxes. Make sure they see it is from you.

2. The subject should be short and sweet. No more than 50 characters. A picture is worth 1,000 words, but not a subject line.

3. Use an email name that your clients will recognize. Is it xyz123@aol or FitForever@aol or better yet Jan@FitForever.

4. Above the fold. You may have heard that term for newspapers. The top stories are above the fold in the newspaper. Don't have your newsletter be too long, and take advantage of the table of contents so your readers can see a snapshot of what is in your newsletter. They can scroll down to the articles of information that interest them.

5. What are you doing to get new clients into your business? Direct mail? Online ads? Newspaper ads? If you are on a limited budget why not use your most valuable asset: your customers. In your newsletter ask your clients to forward your email newsletter to friends and family that may be interested in what your business offers, and ask them to sign up for your email newsletter. You can also start a "bring in a friend" campaign and the email newsletter is a great way to promote it.

6. A footnote to # 5. Email marketing is the most cost-effective direct marketing tool so why not put it at the top of your marketing list whether you have a limited or unlimited budget. Don't take my word for it...

"More than 63% of companies found email marketing the most cost-effective method for customer retention." - Direct Marketing Association

"54% of small businesses surveyed rated email as the top online promotion to drive site visitors and customers to their sites and store fronts." – DMA Interactive

7. Color is key. What is black and white and read all over? A newspaper. That's a great little riddle when we were kids. It is also good advice for your email newsletter. Black font on white background works well. How many of you have been blinded by the "creative" emails that are black background with red or yellow fonts? Need I say more?

8. Never, ever send file attachments. It is a sure-fire way for your message to end up in someone's SPAM folder. This is because unfortunately many of the computer viruses that are started come from attached files. Turn the attached file into a page on your website instead and add a link to it in your newsletter.

9. Watch out for exclamation marks! Don't overuse explanation marks in any written medium, especially in email. The "!" symbol is used as a SPAM filter in many email programs and ISPs (Internet Service Providers).

10. Test before you publish. Always send a test copy of your email newsletter to yourself and your team to make sure things look right once it lands in your inbox. Think of it as a virtual spelling, grammar, and newsletter format checker. And if you added any hyperlinks make sure they work.

Eleven Tips to make sure your Marketing is Local and shared.

1. Have a "Share" button on all your website pages
2. Have a sign up for your enewsletter area on your website
3. Know the writers in your market that can write about you.
4. Offer your writing services to your local papers and magazines that make sense for your business.
5. Become a speaker at a local conference
6. Become a speaker at a national trade association
7. Include a "Share button" in your email marketing campaigns.

8. Thank your customers

9. Ask them for a recommendation or testimonial.

10. Create some buzz around what your customers like about your company. Start a conversation on your Facebook page, your blog, and your enewsletter.

11. Thank your customers (again).

Thank you for buying this book.

Over the years there have been several marketing books that I have enjoyed.

6 Favorite Marketing Books That Made Me Think.

Throughout my career there have been several books I have enjoyed reading that helped increase my knowledge in particular subject matters. These 6 stand out as some I really enjoyed. They helped me think through some things with the role I had at the time, and are great refreshers at any time. You may have others. Which ones have I missed? What are your favorites?

Permission Based Marketing - Turning Strangers Into Friends, and Friends Into Customers by Seth Godin - A quote from this book that stood out for me and has helped me think through every marketing plan I have developed:

Nothing good is free, and that goes double for permission.

Acquiring solid, deep permission from targeted customers in an investment."

Relationship Marketing - Successful Strategies for the Age of the Customer by Regis McKenna - From a guy who was not afraid to tell Steve Jobs to shut up.

You should learn how word of mouth operates in your business and industry, then pass the word."

Blue Ocean Strategy - How to Create Uncontested Market Space and Make the Competition Irrelevant by W.Chan Kim and Renee Mauborgne - This may be looked at as more of a business strategy book. But oh what fun it is to lead marketing as you disrupt an industry.

So great was the blue ocean Ford created that the Model T replaced the horse-drawn carriage as the primary means of transport in the United States."

Digital Leader - 5 Simple Keys To Success And Influence by Erik Qualman - I first heard of Erik not by book but from his excellent video on YouTube Socialnomics. If you have anyone in your company doubting the relevance of social media have them watch it. And yet on the flip side some very good advice:

> *Starting now, pick one day during the week when you will completely unplug from technology."*

BANG! - Getting Your Message Heard In A Noisy World by Linda Kaplan Thaler and Robin Koval. They offer some really creative ideas to get your message heard.

> *Our inner child is where many of our most imaginative and uncensored selves lie. As such, it is an embryonic breeding ground for Big Bang ideas."*

The Art of Social Media - Power Tips for Power Users by Guy Kawasaki and Peg Fitzpatrick. The title is a bit misleading as it is an excellent book for any stage of social media practitioners, beginners and power users.

> *The shelf life of a tweet is 20 minutes."*

There you have it. Six of my favorite marketing books. I highly recommend them all. What are your favorites? and why?

Happy Reading.